Have You Ever Seen an Ant Who Can't?

Have You Ever Seen an Ant Who Can't?

Creepy, Crawly Stings and Wings From God's "Buggy" World

Bernadette McCarver Snyder

Illustrations by Jim Richter

ave maria press Notre Dame, Indiana

Dedication

I dedicate this book to William Daniel Snyder, also known as Will. When Will was born, someone jokingly said, "Will he or won't he?" Through his life, I hope he will AND won't—at the proper times. And, from the fun we've had together, I now know that he WILL always question and explore, amuse and amaze, wander and wonder—as I hope all children will as they and the world discover each other.

© 1999 by Ave Maria Press, Inc.

International Standard Book Number: 0-87793-693-5

Cover and text illustrations by Jim Richter.

Printed and bound in the United States of America.

Library of Congress Cataloging-in-Publication Data

Snyder, Bernadette McCarver.
      Have You Ever Seen an Ant Who Can't : Creepy Crawly Stings and Wings From God's "Buggy" World / Bernadette McCarver Snyder; illustrations by Jim Richter.
          p.   cm.
      Summary: Explores some of the most unusual and remarkable facts about fascinating creatures on and under the earth while also teaching about the loving and imaginative Creator of all.
      ISBN 0-87793-693-5
      1. Insects—Religious aspects—Christianity Juvenile literature. 2. Creation Juvenile literaure. [1. Insects—Religious aspects—Christianity. 2. Creation. 3. Christian life.] I. Richter, Jim, ill. II. Title.
BT746.S573   1999
(231.7'65)—dc21

                    (99-30179)
                        CIP

Contents

Introduction

God Made WHAT?

Creepy, crawly, yucky! Slinky, slimy, eeewh! Hairy, scary! Bug off! You bug me!

Some people do NOT like bugs, insects, or creepy, crawly things with stings or wings—but maybe YOU do! OR maybe you WOULD if you knew more about them and their "secret" lives.

Did you know that God made butterflies who taste with their feet, moths who smell with feathery wires on the tops of their heads, and katydids who have ears on their knees? Did you know there are more than 10 QUINTILLION bugs? Did you know some bugs lay eggs that look like flower pots and some can fly as fast as an airplane and some look like pebbles and some have "jobs" sorta like people?

Some bugs are like architects who design buildings—except the bugs build with pasteboard or clay instead of bricks and cement. Some are like carpenters because they bore holes in wood. Some are like miners because they dig deep, deep underground. And most of them are hunters!

You probably know SOME things about SOME kinds of bugs. You may have seen different bugs in a park or in your backyard—under a rock or on a leaf or in the grass. But do you know how a beetle uses his "elbows" or how a mud dauber builds tunnels or how a butterfly coils her "tongue" under her chin or how a snail "walks" on one foot? Have you ever heard about a dragonfly's eyes or a beetle bug that weighs almost as much as a hamster?

Well, you WILL in this book. So turn the page now and begin to discover the weirdly wonderful, creepy, crawly things with stings and wings in God's fun, fascinating, "buggy" world.

You'll notice that we've made this book in black and white—but if you'd like a more colorful book, there's a note on each page to suggest which colors you could add.

7

Have You Ever Seen an Ant Who Can't?

When God made the ant, he must have forgotten to tell the ANT about the word CAN'T! Since the ant doesn't know you can't pick up something that is bigger than you are, he does! Maybe you've seen a tiny ant, scurrying along, carrying something on his back that is two or three times bigger than he is. He can't do that—but he does! A 200-pound man couldn't put a 600-pound piano on his back and run along, carrying it to his house. But as soon as an ant finds a "treasure" of some kind, whether it's small or waaay too big, he hoists it on his back and hurries along, taking it home to his family.

This ant is a "family" kind of insect—and a very busy one. He and his family like to work together. That's why he is called a worker ant.

But God didn't make just ONE kind of ant. God ALSO made the leaf-cutter ant who grows his own food. This ant cuts up pieces of leaves and stacks them in a heap in his underground nest. His leaf

Worker Ant

heap (like a compost heap) grows a fungus—a fast-food his family likes better than burgers! God ALSO made army ants who march along in a row like soldiers on parade. They stop every once in a while to "camp" and make a temporary nest, stay for a bit, and then march off again. God ALSO made the carpenter ant who—without a tool belt—bores into wooden buildings or rotten tree trunks to make a nest. Yes, God made LOTS of ants— AND aunts.

Do YOU have a favorite aunt? Aunt Susie, Aunt Matilda, Aunt Betty? If you do, maybe you could call or visit her today and tell her about the things you've learned about the different kinds of ants God made.

What will you color the leaf the ant is carrying? Green, of course!

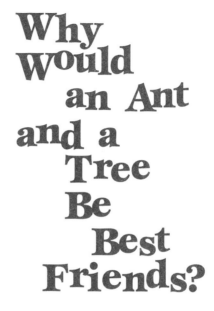

Why Would an Ant and a Tree Be Best Friends?

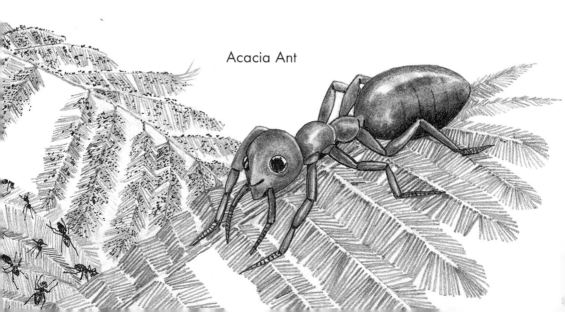

Acacia Ant

Now here's ANOTHER different kind of ant God made—and a very unusual one. This ant lives in an acacia tree and is called the acacia ant. The tree and the ant are best friends because the tree feeds the ant and the ant protects the tree! Now how do you think a tiny ant could protect a tree? Well, it isn't just ONE ant that lives in the tree but SWARMS of ants, and they are always on "enemy alert." If anyone or anything even TOUCHES the tree, the ants leap on to the enemy and use their "sting guns." An acacia ant sting is sorta like a wasp sting OR, as one "enemy" who got stung described it, "like having a staple fired into your cheek." Ouch!

The acacia ants dart up and down the leafy acacia branches, constantly patrolling the tree which is about the size of a large front-yard shrub. In return, the tree is a "Bed and Breakfast" (and Lunch and Dinner!) for the ants. The tree has large thorns that the ants "clear out," tossing sawdust in the air as they dig and tunnel. Once the thorn is removed, making a cozy nest hole, the ants move into their new home. For food, the ants tap into the acacia stems that provide a steady flow of liquid sugar—a yummy drink and dessert all in one! But the ants need a "balanced diet" just like YOU do, so the tree provides that too. The tips of the tree's leaflets have little things that look like tiny golden pears, and these contain the kinds of vitamins, protein, and fat the ants need. The ants watch the pears grow, checking on them every day, and when one is "ripe," an ant will break it off and happily carry it back to the nest for a family feast!

Wasn't it a good idea for God to introduce the ant to the tree so they could become good friends and help each other? Can you think of some way YOU could help a friend—or a relative or a neighbor—today?

Color the acacia tree green.

My, What Big Eyes You Have!

Have you ever read about a scary, fire-breathing dragon in a fairy tale? Well, here's a REAL true-life dragon—the dragonfly. You will NEVER see a dragonfly draggin' around—he moves fast! And would you look at those eyes! God decided to give this buggy flyer buggy eyes that are bigger than the eyes of any other insect. And do you know why they're so big? Well, when YOU look out of YOUR eyes, each eye has one lens to see through—and that's plenty for you to see everything you need to see. But guess what! God put 30,000 lenses in each dragonfly eye! That's why his eyes are so big! The dragonfly NEEDS eyes like that when he goes out shopping for dinner, because he moves sooo fast and has to look sooo fast. The reason he moves so fast is because of those big wings God gave him—wings that let him dart, swoop, zoom, and even fly backward! When his enemies see him coming, they must think he looks as scary as those fairy-tale dragons—but YOU don't have to worry. Dragonflies may look scary, but they NEVER hurt people.

Would you like to have huge eyes with lots of lenses? That might be fun for a while (or maybe on Halloween), but such big buggy eyes fit a

lot better on a big bug
than they would on a small
you. YOUR eyes are a special gift from
God, made to fit you just right. So use
them carefully today and every day—
to wink, to blink, to watch, to work,
OR to be a lookout on a pirate ship, an
Indian scout, or a secret super spy. When
you close your eyes in the daytime,
you can dream of all kinds of pretend
adventures. And when you close your eyes
at night, you can say a goodnight prayer to
tell God thanks for your made-to-order,
just-right eyes.

Dragonfly

Color the dragonfly's body green, his eyes light blue, and the "nose" between his eyes yellow.

Never Rumble With

There are bumblebees, honeybees, worker bees—and they all belong to the same family. One is called a bumblebee because he makes a humming, bumbling sound when he flies. God gave this bee wings and a sting—but he only stings in self-defense if you bother him or if you bother his nest or try to steal his honey! So to keep from getting stung, get your honey at the grocery store and don't rumble with the bumble!

Making honey takes a lot of teamwork—and God taught the bees just what to do. It starts when lots of bees fly out to find flower gardens. From the flowers, they collect two things: they suck up a sweet, sugary liquid called nectar, and they collect balls of powdery pollen on their back legs (so sometimes it looks like they are wearing yellow pollen pants!).

During a summer, these bees may pay over a BILLION

Bumblebee

14

a Bumblebee!

visits to flowers and fly almost two million miles—nearly ten times farther than from the earth to the moon!

The "gathering" bees take the nectar back to the nest, which is called a hive. In this nest there can be as many as 30,000 worker bees (there are more bees in some hives than there are people in some towns!). While some of the worker bees turn the nectar into honey, other busy bees make waxy honeycombs where they can store the honey. Working together as a team—both in and out of the nest—the bees in one hive can make over 100 pounds of honey in one summer! That's a lot of flying, a lot of working, and a lot of honey!

Did you ever watch a bee buzzing around a flower? Did you notice which COLOR flower the bee liked best? Here's an experiment you can try in the summertime (but you might need a grownup to help you). Get some plastic flowers—red, yellow, and blue—and put them outside in the yard. Then make a thick, sweet syrup by mixing together sugar with a bit of hot water. Pour some drops of the syrup on each plastic flower. If you can, watch for bees to come and see which flower they visit first. OR check later to see which flower has LOST the most syrup—and you'll know which color the bees liked best.

Color the bands on the bee yellow and color the flower red.

Meet a Swinger Who's "On the Web" Without a Computer!

This web swinger doesn't NEED a computer because she makes her own web! Yep, it's Miss Spider, who keeps busy every day, spinning and weaving those silken webs. The webs she weaves look very delicate and are sometimes very small, stretching across a tiny corner, and sometimes very large, stretching from one side of a fence to another, like a lacy gate. The web is the spider's shopping bag! She uses it to catch her dinner the way you might use a fishing pole to catch a fish to have for YOUR dinner! And you know what? The silk a spider uses to make a web is thinner than one of the hairs on your head, but it's as STRONG as a piece of steel wire the same size!

God made many different KINDS of spiders. Some are large and scary looking but are really harmless and gentle. Others are smaller but have poison in their bites! And some spiders have unusual names. There's a black widow spider, a crab spider, a raft spider, an ant spider, and a wolf spider! And some spiders sail off to see the world by making themselves a balloon to travel in!

Color the spider brown.

16

How do you think a spider could make a balloon? Well, she climbs up somewhere—like the top of a fence—and spins out a strand of silk. It gets longer and longer until it is caught by a puff of wind. The spider lets go of the post and sails into the air—and then she very quickly grabs the silk with her front feet and spins a tiny basket to sit in. Then she spins out another silk thread as long as the first and the two act like sails to keep her basket flying in the air. Sometimes she flies a long way, over fields, and farms, and even towns. When she's ready to land, she pulls in the two silk threads the way a sailor would take down the sails on a ship, and her basket slowly comes down to land on a nice leaf where she will make her new home.

Doesn't that sound like fun?

Where would YOU like to fly if you could spin a silk balloon? Think about that today. There are so many wonderful places to visit in God's great world—or even in the outer space of God's universe. But one of the best things about traveling in imagination is knowing that you can come home again when it's time for supper!

Spider

17

Is a Caterpillar a Tractor or an Eating Machine?

Have you ever seen men working at a construction site, using all kinds of really BIG machines? One of those machines was probably a "Caterpillar" tractor. This Caterpillar tractor is used to go across rough ground, so instead of having wheels like a car, it moves on metal belts that roll along under it—the same way an army tank moves. If you haven't seen one of those big machines, maybe you've seen a TOY Caterpillar tractor. And you have probably also seen the INSECT that is named a caterpillar. The machine and the insect may have the same name because of the way they move along—BUT there is a big difference.

The fuzzy wuzzy caterpillar you might find on a leaf in your backyard is an EATING machine—and she has a secret. This caterpillar eats ALL the time, chewing on leaves and flower buds from morning until night. If YOU had to chew all the time, your jaws would get very tired, wouldn't they? But maybe that's because you have only one set of jaws. God gave the caterpillar TWO sets of jaws! One set works up and down the same way yours does, but the other set works sideways. This helps the caterpillar chew non-stop. So the

18

caterpillar gets fatter and fatter and fatter until she looks like she will burst—and she does! She bursts right out of her skin! But it's OK because she has already grown another, bigger skin so she has room to keep right on eating!

The caterpillar keeps eating and bursting and filling up her new skin until finally something happens that seems like magic— and that's her secret! You probably already know the caterpillar's secret, but turn the page and you might be surprised to learn some things that you DIDN'T already know!

There are lots of different KINDS of caterpillars, and they are all different colors. (Sometimes people even use caterpillars to predict the weather, depending on their color and how fuzzy they are!) Why don't you color this one with stripes of yellow and black?

Caterpillar

19

How Could a Fuzzy Eating Machine Turn Into a Fancy Flying Machine?

Yep, just as you expected, after the caterpillar skin bursts for the last time, she turns into something really funny looking that also has a funny name. It's called a chrysalis. And when the chrysalis splits open, the fuzzy wuzzy crawling caterpillar has magically turned into a beautiful flying butterfly. Don't you think God had a great idea the day he created the caterpillar/butterfly?

There are LOTS of different kinds of butterflies, in ALL kinds of colors. The smallest butterfly is called the dwarf blue and each of her wings is about the size of your little fingernail. The largest butterfly is called the Queen Alexandra's birdwing—and her wings are as wide as this book is long!

The caterpillar isn't the only one with a secret—the butterfly has some too! She has a sipper-straw kind of "tongue" that's called a proboscis. She uses it like a straw to sip nectar from flowers the way you use a straw to sip a cool drink from a glass! But when she is finished sipping, she can curl her long "straw" up under her chin! And here's another surprise: when the butterfly lights on a flower, she knows right away if it has the sweet nectar she likes. And do you know HOW she knows? Because God put tastebuds on the butterfly's feet!

Since there are so many different kinds of butterflies, color this one whichever colors you like best.

The next time you see a butterfly, you can see how beautiful she is as she flutters from flower to flower, but you will also know her secrets—that she has a straw-tongue curled up under her chin and tastebuds on her feet!

The next time you meet someone new who you think you might not like, don't be too quick to judge. This "caterpillar" might turn out to have as many nice secrets and be just as interesting as the beautiful butterfly.

Butterfly

Cricket

Who Would Use a Bug for a Watchdog?

On summer evenings, you might hear crickets "tuning up" in the grass to begin a little night music—a chirping serenade. When they rub their wings together, they make "music" that people like, but most people would NOT pick one of these chirpers for a pet. They would choose a puppy or a kitty cat. However, in ancient China, people loved the cheery chirping sound of a cricket SO much, they made little bamboo cages and kept singing crickets in them as pets! Many of those cages were very beautiful, decorated with precious ivory or jade, and today some museums have collections of those ancient cricket cages on display—without the crickets.

Since the Chinese usually had a pet cricket in the house, they used him the way YOU might use a watchdog. If you had a dog in your house, he would probably bark if someone tried to get into your house at night—and the noise would wake you up so you could protect yourself. But the Chinese used a cricket in just the OPPOSITE way! The cricket chirped ALL night—UNLESS a stranger came near. The Chinese would put the cricket cage under the bed and if a burglar came in the night, the cricket would STOP chirping. The owner had gotten so used to the chirping that the sudden silence would wake him up! (Just like you get so used to hearing the TV, you notice when the sound suddenly stops.)

The people in England don't keep crickets for pets, but they DO play a GAME called cricket—with bats and a ball—and it's so popular, hundreds of people come to watch like they might watch an American baseball game. Maybe because of this game, the word "cricket" has come to mean "playing fair." Today if someone does something that is not right or not fair, someone else might say, "That's not cricket!"

Would you like to have a cricket for a pet or for a watchdog? Or would you like to play a game of cricket? The next time you play ANY kind of game, remember the little singing cricket and always play fair so you will never have someone say to YOU, "That's not cricket!"

Color the cricket grayish green with a red eye.

Where Would You Send Mail to a Snail?

The post office would have a hard time delivering a letter to a snail's house because the snail takes her house with her wherever she goes! Just like a turtle, the snail carries her house along on her back. No matter how far she travels, she's still in her house—so a snail never has to hurry home for dinner! YOU may have to hurry home for a dinner but a snail never does—and it's a good thing because a snail moves sooooo slowly, she NEVER hurries!

Maybe that's why God gave her that ready-to-go house! God also gave the snail two horns and one foot! The snail's eyes are at the end of her two "horns" so she can look up and around to see where she's going—and if she sees something that scares her, she can pull her eyes right back inside her head! The snail uses her one foot to slowly pull herself and glide along— and wherever she goes, she leaves a little oozy, silvery trail. That ooze comes out of her body whenever she moves—and you know why? It protects her foot so it won't get scratches from the ground!

Color the snail's head green and put yellow stripes on her shell house.

Wasn't it nice of God to give her some ooze for her moves? When YOU get a scratch on your foot, you can put some oozy cream on it to heal it, but the snail doesn't have to—her ooze is built in!

Do you ever move sloooowly like a snail when you are supposed to be getting ready to go somewhere or supposed to be cleaning up something you left right in the middle of the floor? Well, God gave you TWO feet instead of one, so maybe you should start trying to move faster! Why don't you pretend today that you are following a snail trail—and pick up all the "trails" of toys and games you have left somewhere? Maybe you could even make snail-trailing one of the things you do EVERY day!

Snail

That's Not Just a Stick—It's a Walking Stick!

When people go hiking in the mountains or the woods, they often take along something to help them over rough spots—a sturdy "walking stick."

But on their hike, they might pass right by a LIVING walking stick and never see him! God made this insect with a long skinny green or brown body that looks just like a leafless twig of a tree. During the day, the walking stick keeps very quiet clinging to a plant, with only his long, thin legs swaying gently as though they are

Walking Stick

being blown by the breeze—and he looks just like "one of the gang" of twigs in the garden. Hungry birds who like to eat insects pass right by—just like the hikers—and never see the walking stick. He is so still, it seems like he's in a trance or a coma. Even if you touch him, he doesn't move. But wait until night comes. Wait until the birds and the hikers have gone to sleep. THEN the little walking stick will start moving and, in the safe darkness of the night, he'll go looking for some juicy fresh leaves to have for his supper.

Have you ever noticed how SOME people move around a lot, make a lot of noise or a lot of trouble, and always seem to be ready to fuss or fight? Maybe they think if they act "big," nobody will bother them. But the little walking stick does just the opposite. He doesn't want his enemies to notice him, so he just lays low and keeps quiet.

Which way do YOU think is the best way—to try to act big or to lay low? It's never good to act big just to cause trouble, but sometimes you might need to speak up so people won't think you're just a stick!

Think today of times when it's important to keep quiet—and times when you need to speak up. Then say a prayer, asking God to help you always choose the BEST way.

Color the walking stick green or brown.

Better Look Where You're Walking!

Some day you might be walking along in the grass and suddenly—right next to your foot!—a big green bug will surprise you by leaping up and away. If you try to catch him, he will KEEP leaping away—always faster than you expect. Well, that bug has a name that fits what he DOES. His name is grasshopper.

A grasshopper, hopping in the grass, is VERY hard to catch. That's because he can hop SO high and leap SO far. He can leap two or three or four times farther than his body is long! Can YOU hop that high and leap that far? You might THINK you can, but think about this—you are LOTS "longer" than the grasshopper is, so you would have to leap much, much farther than he does to get even. God did NOT make your legs for that kind of hopping. If God had given YOU the kind of legs he gave the grasshopper, you could probably leap right over your house!

When the grasshopper isn't hopping, he makes a chirping sound by rubbing his legs against his wings. But he makes a DIFFERENT sound when he flies. This is the kind of sound you may have heard somewhere else. Have you ever seen a boy put playing cards in the spokes of his bike's wheels and then ride down the street really fast?

Color the grasshopper green.

When the wind hits the cards, you hear a click-clacking, clattering noise that sounds a lot like the grasshopper's flying sound.

Why don't you pretend to be a grasshopper today and find out how high and how far you can hop in the grass (but don't try to hop over your house!). OR—if you have a bike (or if a friend has one)—you could try putting some playing cards in the spokes of the bike's wheels and ride around, click-clacking like a flying grasshopper!

Grasshopper

Have You Ever Seen a

This bug probably ISN'T praying, but she IS one of the most unusual insects God made. Do you know WHY she's called a praying mantis? Well, according to legend, many, many years ago in the land of Greece, a peasant saw this insect in the grass—and he thought it was a very strange sight indeed. He had never seen anything like it before. The insect was standing up on her back legs, with her green shimmery wings floating behind her like a veil—and her front legs were lifted up in the air, the way a lady might stand with her arms lifted up to heaven, praying. The peasant thought the insect looked like a religious person so he named her mantis (a Greek word which means "prophet")—and ever after, she has been known as the praying mantis.

The six-legged mantis is usually about two and one-half inches long, which is very "tall" for an insect. So she looks more scary than prayerful when she "stands up," raises her wings, and hisses to scare off an enemy. The mantis usually lives in a meadow or on flowers, so you might see one somewhere some time this summer.

Unlike the mantis, most people pray kneeling down, with their hands folded together. Is that how YOU say your prayers at bedtime? Today, why don't you pretend you are a praying mantis? Go out in the yard, stand tall, and lift your arms up to heaven. Look up at the sky or close your eyes and think about God. Talk to God. Then listen. And just maybe you will feel like you hear God talking back to you.

Color the praying mantis green and light brown.

Bug Praying?

Praying Mantis

This scary looking fellow is called the trap-door spider. He is a

Look Who's Peeking Out That Trap Door!

smart and sneaky guy who likes to "order in" instead of going OUT to dinner! Sooo he uses his fangs (or claws) to dig a deep hole in the ground for a snug nest and lines it with the silk he spins. Then he adds a lid—or a "trap door"—to fit on top of the hole. The sly spider sits in his cozy nest, peeking out, watching and waiting like a super spy with binoculars. He isn't spying though. He's just waiting for his dinner to be delivered! He watches and waits, until something crawls by that looks like what a hungry spider would order (no pizza for this guy!). Then up pops the spider out of his trap door—like a jack-in-the-box—and grabs his dinner!

This trap-door builder is just one of the MANY kinds of interesting spiders God made. Did you know scientists have identified about 34,000 different kinds of spiders living on earth? And there are probably many more different kinds living in webs somewhere that the scientists haven't found yet. (Maybe if YOU become a

scientist some day, you'll discover some of them!) All of the spiders belong to the ARACHNID family (pronounced uh-RAK-nid).

Color the spider brown.

32

Have YOU ever hidden in or behind or under something—like the trap-door spider—and then jumped out to surprise someone? You probably have. Now here's a riddle you can use to surprise somebody else! Question: What SECRET are all of these insects hiding—a beetle, a butterfly, and a walking stick? Answer: Each insect has a name that contains the name of ANOTHER insect. The BEEtle is hiding a bee . . . the butterFLY is hiding a fly . . . and the walking sTICK is hiding a tick!

You can play this game with a friend, using other animals and insects God made. An elephant has an ant inside . . . a mongoose has a goose inside . . . a beagle has an eagle inside. How many more secrets do you think are hiding in the world God made? See how many you can find!

Trap-Door Spider

33

Ladybug, Ladybug,

The little red ladybug is probably the most popular of all the insects. And do you know why? Because she has an appetite for aphids! This makes her a friend of gardeners and farmers. You see, aphids are tiny bugs that suck the juice out of plants and kill them—

Ladybug

Fly Away Home...

until along comes the ladybug, in her red Superwoman cape, to eat up the aphids and save the garden.

God made the ladybug so tiny, she could probably fit on your fingernail. She's little but powerful (like you!). And God decorated her round shiny red body with big black dots so you will recognize her right away if you ever see her sitting on a leaf.

There's an old sing-song saying about a ladybug that you might have heard. It goes, "Ladybug, ladybug, fly away home . . . your house is on fire, your children will burn." Do you wonder where "home" is for a ladybug and why her children might burn? Well, as you know, a ladybug and her children live and work on plants and vines—and it was once the custom at the end of summer for farmers to burn the old vines to clear their fields for the next year. Soooo . . . if there were any little ladybugs still in the vines, they were in danger. Maybe someone somewhere saw a ladybug in the garden at the same time a field was burning and said the sing-song to her. It doesn't make much sense now, but people are still saying it to ladybugs today. Do you know any other silly sing-songs, like, "Ring around the rosy, pocket full of posies . . ."?

Maybe you could make up some of your OWN sing-songs or poems today. Let's start with a new one for the ladybug. How about—"God gave ladybugs red capes with black DOTS. . . . He put them in gardens and other leafy SPOTS. . . . And gardeners like them lots and lots and LOTS. . . ."

Color the ladybug's Superwoman cape red.

Now it's YOUR turn to think of a sing-song about something God made!

How Far Can a Butterfly Fly?

Monarch
Butterfly

Some people like to stay home, some like to travel. It's the same with butterflies. Some of these beautiful, fragile flyers flutter around only one neighborhood—but then there's the monarch butterfly. God "programmed" this butterfly with a mysterious desire to travel—far, far away. At the end of every summer, as the weather begins to cool, thousands of monarch butterflies leave North America and fly as far as two thousand miles to get to the warmth of Mexico. They travel from far-flung places like Michigan, Illinois, Maryland, Kansas, Nebraska, Iowa, Missouri, Wisconsin, Indiana, Ohio—and maybe YOUR backyard.

Gliding on the wind, some travel as far as eighty miles a day. As they near Mexico, coming from many different directions, thousands of them gather in the air, with their brown and honey-yellow wings fluttering, until the sky looks like it is filled with dark clouds. Then the butterflies swoop down and fill the branches of trees, the way you might fill the branches of your Christmas tree with pretty ornaments.

In the spring, the monarchs head back where they started, looking for fields of milkweed—their favorite food. (They like milkweed so much, they are sometimes called the milkweed butterfly.) But as the summer ends, the monarch journey begins again.

Are you one of the "butterflies" who likes to stay near home? Or did God program YOU with the wish to travel to far-away places? It can be a lot of fun to travel, but it's also nice to be snug at home—and

Color the butterfly wings honey-yellow with dark brown edges around the white dots.

maybe the best of all is to try a little bit of both. Isn't it nice to know that, for the rest of your life, whether you stay at home or fly away, you will never have to be lonely— because God will always be flying along with you!

A Bug in a Knight's Suit of Armor

The scorpion has a hard shell that looks a bit like he's wearing a suit of armor. But do you know what? That's the scorpion's skeleton! You wear YOUR skeleton on the INSIDE, but the scorpion is one of many creatures God made with the skeleton on the OUTSIDE! This armor is, of course, made to protect the scorpion from

Scorpion

his enemies. And he's not only armed, he's also dangerous—the scorpion has a poison dart hidden in that armor!

There are 600 different kinds of scorpions and all of them have a poison stinger at the tip of their tail. A scorpion who lives in the Sahara Desert must need to protect himself from LOTS of enemies because HE has enough poison in his tail-stinger to kill a dog in a few minutes or a person in a few hours!

Don't worry though—the scorpion doesn't attack unless he's attacked. In fact, he usually stays hidden during the day—under rocks or old logs—and only comes out at night to look for food.

Would YOU like to have a suit of armor—OR wear your skeleton on the OUTSIDE? It might be fun to have a suit of armor so you could pretend you are a knight named Sir Lancelot or Sir Runalot, but armor would get verrry heavy if you had to wear it every day. And you

Color the scorpion orange.

wouldn't look too good if you had to wear your skeleton on the outside! So maybe today you could resolve to be Sir Thanksalot and always remember to thank everybody who helps you—friends, family, teachers, and especially God, who put your skeleton on the INSIDE!

This Beetle Bats a Ball Backward!

The dung beetle has a very strange way of grocery shopping. He uses his "elbows" to sweep a space, flinging aside all the things he doesn't want. Then he gathers up "armfuls" of the food he has chosen, rakes it underneath his back legs, and uses his body to press it together. He spins it around and around with his hind legs until it forms a perfect ball. He adds food until a small ball grows to the size of a walnut and then to the size of an apple—or even larger. Now he's ready to take it home. He puts his head down and his rear end up and begins to push the ball BACKWARD with his hind feet! He doesn't even try to find an easy path. Sometimes he pushes the ball UP a hill and if he loses his grip, it rolls back down, and he goes tumbling down with it (which is the reason he is sometimes called a tumblebug). But that doesn't discourage him! He just starts pushing his ball back up. Even if he has to start over ten or twenty times, he never gives up.

Color the beetle's ball whatever color you think it might be.

40

Sometimes another beetle comes along and PRETENDS to want to help him roll the ball along—but then tries to steal it. They wrestle, and sometimes the thief wins and goes off with the ball and the first beetle has to start all over again! But finally he manages to get his ball of food to wherever he wanted to go. Then he digs a hole for himself, using his sharp forehead and feet, hurling sand behind him. He stores the ball in his burrow, and it almost fills up his whole room, from floor to ceiling! He hops in and covers the opening with some trash and settles down for a loooong banquet.

When God made this beetle, he gave him lots of stick-to-it-iveness! No matter what happens to discourage him, he just gets up and starts all over again. The next time YOU get discouraged, remember the dung beetle and just start all over again—even if you have to bat your ball backward!

Dung Beetle

Meet a Hairy, Scary Frisbee

Oh yeah, he's bad. He's hairy. He's scary. He's a bug as big as a frisbee. He's just a spider, but he's big enough to eat small birds for dinner! That's why he's called the bird-eating tarantula.

But guess what! This bad bug is near-sighted—and he's too fuzzy to wear glasses! So he feels his way around, prowling the forest floor at night, hunting for something to eat. He usually eats insects, but sometimes he even catches and eats little birds. This tarantula is so big, he doesn't weave a web and sit in it like other spiders. Instead, he just sneaks around the forests of South America—so you probably won't meet one unless you find one in the bug house at the zoo.

As you probably guessed, the tarantula is the BIGGEST of all the spiders. God made several different KINDS of tarantulas and, since they don't have good eyesight, he put poison in their bites so they can protect themselves from enemies even BIGGER than they are!

There's a once-upon-a-time story about the EUROPEAN tarantula. People once thought that if you were bitten by one of these spiders, you would get a strange disease called "tarantism." You would not sneeze or cough or get a fever, but you would feel sad and droopy—AND you would have an uncontrollable desire to DANCE! Now there is a lively dance called the tarantella, so maybe if you tangled with a tarantula, you would dance the tarantella!

A poison tarantula's bite is NOT funny—but the idea of a spider making you want to dance DOES seem funny! Do YOU like to dance? Do you like to WATCH people dance? You might not want to learn how to do fancy dances, but when you hear music it's fun to twirl around with the rhythm AND it's fun to run and leap and dance through the water of a sprinkler in the summertime. So tell God thanks today for tarantulas and the tarantella and legs that can leap and dance.

Color the tarantula brown with yellow spots on his fuzzy legs.

Tarantula

Leaf Insect

This Is a Crawler Wearing Camouflage

Have you ever seen a soldier wearing a camouflage uniform? The uniform is made just like regular clothes except instead of being a solid color like blue or brown, the fabric is a strange pattern of greens and browns and shadowy shapes, so it looks like trees in a jungle or forest. Soldiers wear clothes like this when they are going to be IN a jungle or forest—so the enemy will not be able to see them. (Today some people like these clothes so much, they wear camouflage hats or jackets even though they're not soldiers.)

Insects like to wear camouflage too.

And God made several insects that look just like the place where they live—so enemies cannot see them. One of the most amazing look-alikes is the leaf insect. God made her to look JUST LIKE the leaves she lives on! She's pale green like a leaf. Her body is shaped like a leaf. Each of her legs looks like a leaf. And when she lays eggs, her eggs look like flower seeds!

She is REALLY in disguise—and she looks very pretty that way. Did YOU ever wear a disguise? Maybe you might like to wear a disguise today! You could wear a false mustache or a beard or a funny mask or dress up like a clown or a princess or a pirate! It can be a lot of fun to wear a disguise and make yourself look like somebody else. Actors and actresses do that all the time—wearing wigs and different clothes and makeup. They are very good at making themselves look like someone they are NOT. But only GOD could make a bug look like a leaf!

Color the leaf insect green, of course, of course.

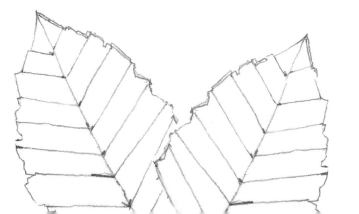

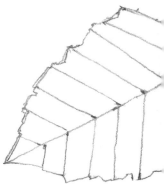

Look Out!
It's Mighty Bite!

You'll hear her coming before you see her . . . hummmm . . . whine . . . zoom. Mighty bite lands on YOU—and gives you a mosquito bite. Ouch! Itch!

Mosquitoes must like people a lot—because they are always taking bites out of them. Or maybe they just like the TASTE of people! This is one bug that is NOT easy to pick for a friend. But God must love them, even if people don't.

The mosquito lays her eggs on the surface of water or on water plants. When the eggs hatch, the new mosquitoes fly off—hummmm . . . whine . . . zoom—looking for somebody to bite! And God taught the mosquito to fly sooo fast! When you hear the whine, that's the sound of her wings flapping. A mosquito can flap her wings about 600 times in the same amount of time it would take YOU to slowly say the word "mosquito"!

You might not like the way a mosquito bites, but you sure can't beat the way she flies! And she IS an interesting LOOKING insect with her big eyes and little "nose."

Sometimes it's hard to understand the reason for something that's a nuisance to you—like the mosquito or a chore you don't like to do. Sometimes you might wonder, "What good is it anyway?" But God has a reason for everything he makes, and a

Color the tummy of the mosquito red and her wings gray.

mosquito is an important part of God's universe, just like every insect, every animal, every human. Just like YOU are. Maybe . . . just maybe . . . sometimes when you misbehave, you are a nuisance too.

But God made YOU for a reason, and God loves you!

Mosquito

What do a horse, a house, a robber, a dance, and a fruit have in common? Well, they're all names of different kinds of flies. The one you probably know best is the housefly because you might have seen it flitting around your house or yard in the summertime. But if you live on a farm or have ridden horses, you might also have seen the horsefly.

The horsefly is different from other flies because she does NOT make a buzzing noise when she flies. This helps her silently sneak up

A Horse That Can Walk on the Ceiling!

Horsefly

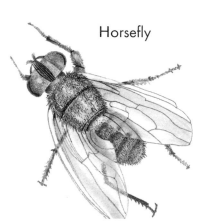

on a large animal—like a horse—and he doesn't know what's coming! What's coming is a hypodermic needle! The lady horsefly sticks her "needle nose" into the horse and sucks out some of his blood! She doesn't do it to be mean, though. The horse is big and she is small, and she just needs a little bit of his blood to make eggs so she can have baby flies. (The LADY fly is the only "blood sucker" in her family. Her husband is a VEGETARIAN. The gentleman fly eats only fruit and juices from flowers!)

And you know what? The fly can climb up a wall or walk on the ceiling. That's because God made fly feet with glue guns in them! At the end of each foot, the fly has little hollow hairs she can use to shoot out some sticky fluid whenever she

48

needs to hold on to a smooth surface. This means she can hang on to the ceiling, upside down, for however long she wants. Maybe if you were as small and light as a fly and had glue on your feet, you could hang from a ceiling too! Wouldn't that be fun? Now what about the other flies God made? Well, the fruit fly likes to eat fruit. The robber fly chases and catches other insects in the air. And dance flies gather in swarms and fly up and down like they are dancing.

These flies are all from the same family, but they look different, act different, like different foods, and have different names. Does that sound like the people in YOUR family? God made each of you different and special, from your fingerprints to the smile on your face. Wasn't that a good idea!

Color the fly's eyes green and the needle-nose orange.

Tell God thanks today for making you YOU— even if you can't walk on the ceiling!

The Mud Pie Maker

Did you ever make mud pies or play in a mud puddle? Well, here's an insect who is a mud pie-maker—but she isn't playing. She's working. This is a wasp who is called a mud dauber because she makes her nest out of mud. If you look around in the summer, you might see a big blob of mud stuck on the side of a building—and that will probably be the messy-looking but snug-as-a-bug nest of a mud dauber.

The mud dauber picks out a place to build her nest, and then she goes to the nearest mudhole or to the muddy bank of a pond or stream. She runs back and forth, digging in the mud here and there, looking for just the right kind of mud. Suddenly, she pushes her nose right into the mud and looks like she's standing on her head, with her tummy waving in the air. She takes out a bit of mud and flies to her new "home site" and sticks the mud on the wall—the way a cement worker might start to build a sidewalk.

The little wasp keeps making trips, adding mud until she has a big blob. Then she digs a tunnel in the mud like a long hall and works on the walls of the hall until they are very smooth—just like a

Mud Dauber

cement worker smoothes out concrete, using a tool called a trowel. The mud dauber doesn't have a trowel, but God made her jaws in a special way so she can USE them like a trowel! When the hall is finished, she fills it with food, lays an egg in it, and seals it up. She makes more halls and lays more eggs and then covers the whole nest by messily slapping on more mud. She doesn't worry about smoothing the OUTSIDE of the house to look good. She just wants the INSIDE to have smooth, cozy cribs for her babies.

Have you noticed that some PEOPLE have houses that look messy on the outside but are very nice on the inside—OR look nice on the outside but are messy inside? Have you noticed that some people look very good on the outside but might not be very nice inside?

Think about that today. Which side do you think God sees as MOST important—the outside or the inside?

Color the mud dauber's mud the color of mud!

How Many Inches

There are twelve inches in a foot, but who knows how many inches there are in an inchworm? You've probably noticed that there are all kinds of squiggly worms wiggling around under or over the ground, but this one is called an inchworm—OR a measuring worm—for a very good reason. When she crawls along, she looks like she is "measuring" the ground in inches. She stretches out her front, then pulls her rear along until she rises up in the middle—making a shape like an arch or a rainbow. Then she stretches, pulls, and becomes a rainbow again. Didn't God make this creepy-crawly worm move in an interesting way? Could YOU move like that—stretching out on the ground, then pulling up until your middle makes a rainbow shape?

There is a funny old story that says if you see an inchworm "inching" along on your shirt or sock, it's a good luck sign. Why? She

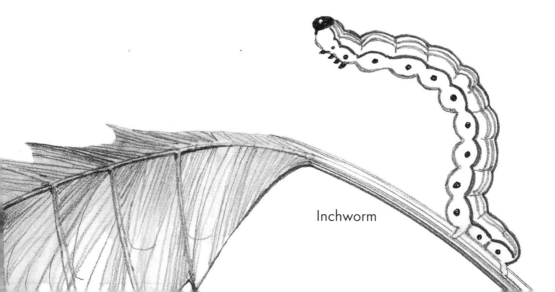

Inchworm

in a Worm?

is supposed to be "measuring"
you to see what size you are—
because you are going to get a NEW
shirt or sock!

If you have a measuring tape in your house, how
about measuring some things today? How long IS an inch?
(It's not very long, is it?) How long is your foot? How big is your head
from ear to ear? How long is your arm or your leg or your thumb?
How far is it from your bed to the refrigerator?

Now here's something else you can measure.
How much do you love God? How LONG do you
spend each day saying a prayer to TELL God how
much you love him?

Color the inchworm pale green.

Have You Ever Seen a Bug Blow Bubbles?

Insects build houses using some VERY strange things—wax, mud, sand, or old logs—but THIS insect builds one of the strangest houses of all. This is the froghopper—and her house is made of bubbles!

This teeny tiny bug builds a house of bubbles that is a whole lot bigger than she is (just like YOUR house is a whole lot bigger than YOU are). But how does she do it? She doesn't even have any soap or a bubble blower!

If YOU tried to make a house of bubbles for yourself—a house much bigger than you are—you would have to use LOTS of bubble soap and work for a LOOOONG time. But the froghopper builds her house quickly—and here's how she does it. Since she lives near water—like a pond or a lake—there are lots of juicy weeds and grasses in her neighborhood. So she climbs up and sticks her beak into a blade of grass or a weed and sucks juice from the plant into her body. She keeps sucking until she is SOOO full of juice that bubbles start to ooze out of her body! Soon she is completely covered with a blob of bubbles—and there she stays, day after day, snug in her bubble house.

But her work is not over. If the sunshine or the wind starts to dry up the bubbles, she gets busy and blows some more. And if it's a sunny or windy day, the froghopper may spend all day blowing bubbles!

Who would think God would teach a bug to blow bubbles? But he did!

What has God taught YOU how to do?

God DID NOT teach YOUR body how to blow froghopper-bubbles—so don't try sucking up juice until you are TOO full! But God DID teach you something. He gave you commandments to teach you how to live a good life. And THEN he gave you a brain and imagination and eyes and ears and arms and legs— and love. With all those gifts he gave you, you can learn to do almost ANYTHING you want to do! What would you MOST like to learn to do this year?

Color some pale pink and blue spots in the froghopper's bubbles.

Froghopper

Firefly

Who's Got the Flashlight?

They're magic! They're mysterious! They're fun! They're fireflies. There are 100 different kinds of this flying bug—and they all carry flashlights. God gave some fireflies a yellow light and some a green light— but he didn't give ANY a red light! He also gave each kind of firefly a different "code" to flash on and off to talk to each other.

In the summertime, if you go out in the yard after dark, you might see those little flashes of light in the grass or in the bushes. And if you ever go to Malaysia, you can go to a riverbank and see quite a sight. The fireflies who live there gather at night in bushes or trees and they ALL flash their lights on and off at the same time—like the flashing lights you see decorating trees and bushes at Christmastime!

In some areas, the firefly is called a lightning bug—although it certainly isn't as bright or as dangerous as a lightning BOLT. (Did you know one bolt of lightning has enough electricity in it to power a 100-watt light bulb in your house for THREE months?) The bug is a lot better to have in your backyard than a bolt because you could never catch a lightning bolt, but you CAN catch a lightning bug! In fact, before people had electricity in their houses, they would sometimes catch lightning bugs and put them in a glass jar—and read by the green or yellow light of the bugs!

Did YOU ever try to catch lightning bugs? If you didn't, why don't you? All you need is a clear glass jar that has a screw-on lid. Punch some air holes in the lid and then, on a summer evening, when it's just beginning to get dark, watch for the blinking lights. Try to catch one firefly in the jar and then slap on the lid. Then try to catch another one. If you catch enough, you can have your own hand-made, God-made lantern. (But let the fireflies go free before you go to bed so they can fly off and blink their flashlight codes for somebody else.)

Color the firefly's tail green or yellow.

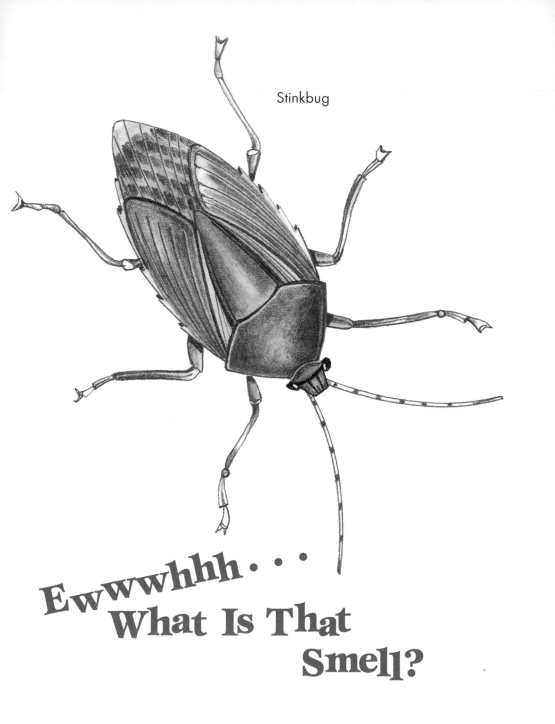

Stinkbug

Ewwwhhh...
What Is That
Smell?

Did you know God made a stinkbug? Yes, he did!

This little bug looks and acts just like a regular bug—unless he gets scared or sees an enemy coming. THEN he uses the "ammunition" God gave him to protect himself. He lets off a terrible stink!

It seems like someone could have given this bug a more interesting name—like the "UNperfumed bug," the "I've-got-a-secret bug," the "hold-your-nose bug," or the "don't-get-any-closer bug." But whoever named this bug must have said, "I calls it like I sees it," and named him the STINKBUG.

Of course, the stinkbug isn't the ONLY insect who protects himself by using the power of odor. There are several others, including the bombardier beetle. This bug fires off a BAAD-smelling chemical spray that EXPLODES when it hits the air, like a small bomb. He has a double-barreled defense, mixing odor AND noise! And someone gave him an exciting name too—the bombardier beetle sounds a lot better than the stinkbug!

Do you know anyone who has a name you don't like? Or what about your OWN name? Do you like it, or do you wish you had a different name? If you DID pick out a new name for yourself, what would it be? Think about that today—and THEN think about your favorite name for God. Is it Protector . . . Creator . . . All-powerful . . . All-loving . . . Father . . . Friend . . . ?

Color the stinkbug green.

Having 2 Left Feet Is Bad— Having 200 Left Feet Is Really Bad!

When somebody is a bad dancer or is clumsy and always tripping over something or falling into something, you might tease them by saying, "You must have two left feet." If you wanted to tease this bug, you would have to say, "You must have 200 left feet." That's because this is a centipede, a bug with LOTS of feet!

His name is a combination of "centi," meaning "100," and "pede," meaning "foot." God probably didn't give the centipede 100 feet, but he did give him so MANY feet that the person who named him must have thought he LOOKED like he had 100 feet.

It would be really funny to watch a centipede try to dance the hokey-pokey. Do you know how that dance goes? "Put your right foot in, put your right foot out, put your right foot in and shake it all about. . . ." The centipede would have to shake so much, he

Centipede

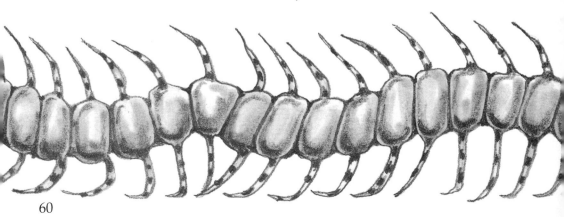

might trip over his own left feet! There once was a poem about the centipede that went something like this:

The centipede was dancing when somebody asked in FUN . . .
With all those feet, which do you shake after which?
This surprised the centipede and he tripped and fell into a ditch.
He was so embarrassed, he began to twitch!
Then he laughed and gave thanks he had 100 feet instead of NONE!

Did YOU ever know exactly how to do something—until someone asked you to do it? Did you ever know the answer to a question or the words to a poem until someone asked you to tell them? All of a sudden, you got tripped up or tongue-tied. You got embarrassed. You felt like falling into a ditch!

That happens to EVERYBODY some time, so the next time that happens, don't be embarrassed or feel like

Color the centipede a pinkish orange.

you have two left feet. Just laugh it off, and ask God to help your feet—or your brain—to do better NEXT time.

Why Would a Wasp Have a Paper Umbrella?

Many years ago, some very smart people made an amazing discovery. They figured out how to use wood to make paper! Who could imagine making a piece of paper for writing a grocery list by first chopping down a tree? But that's how paper is still made today. An even more amazing thing is that a little insect named the paper wasp knew how to make paper BEFORE people did. And guess what—God taught this insect how to make paper that is even BETTER than people-paper!

Now how do you guess the paper wasp does it? First she pulls off shreds of wood from a dead tree trunk or an old fence post. When she has as much wood as she can hold in her mouth, she starts to CHEW. She chews and chews until the wood turns into "pulp," the same kind of mixture people use to make paper, by grinding wood and mixing it with water. The wasp flies back and forth, getting wood, chewing, and using the pulp to form a very fancy nest. When she is finished, she has a nest that looks a lot like a paper umbrella without a handle!

Paper Wasp

But it's even BETTER than a paper umbrella. God gave the paper wasp a special kind of sticky saliva in her mouth and that mixes with the wood as she chews—and that makes her paper WATERPROOF! When rains and storms come along, her paper house does not come apart—so it is much better than a people-paper umbrella would be!

If YOU went out in the rain with a paper umbrella, do you think you would get wet? If you don't have a paper umbrella, the next time a big rain comes along, take a piece of newspaper and hold it over your head and go out in the rain. What do you think will happen?

Tell God thanks today for putting so many interesting things in the world for you to discover—like this wasp who can make a waterproof paper umbrella!

A wasp umbrella is not very colorful, so why don't you color this one your favorite umbrella color!

The Good News/Bad News Bugs

You would NOT want to see any of these bugs near your house. Termites really like to chew on wood, and they could chew up the wood in your house before you even knew they had moved in. That's the bad news. But the GOOD NEWS is that they play a very important part in the ecology of some parts of the world. And guess what— these good news/bad news bugs sometimes live in high-rise condos!

Yep, God taught termites how to build nests that can be as tall as a two-story house! Just like a condo, these tall nests have lots of "rooms" inside and an air circulation system that works like an air conditioner. Termites build their houses out of sand, spit, and mud, and

Termite

the walls are so hard that sometimes the only way you can knock one down is to blow it up with explosives! Can you imagine tiny bugs knowing how to build such a tall, strong nest?

Would you like to play a good news/bad news game today? Get your folks or a friend to help you look through the newspaper and find some GOOD news stories and some BAD news stories—then try to figure out what the people in the BAD news stories could have done to turn them into GOOD news stories. And then think about how you and God could work together to change one of your bad habits into a good habit!

Color the termite house the color of sand.

Would a Worm Use

Most worms do NOT have a feather duster—but THIS one has
something that LOOKS like one! Have you ever SEEN a feather
duster? It's a bunch of feathers attached to the end of a stick. Years
ago, someone got the good idea to make one and use it to dust high
places or little places or corners of the house. Today, although they're
still called FEATHER dusters, some are made of something different—
like nylon strips stuck on a stick. Well, this worm's feather duster is
ALSO made of something different.

She lives in the mud or sand near water and has a very fancy
name—and a very fancy decoration! She is named a eupolymnia
nebulosa (you-po-lim-neeah neb-you-low-sah.) When God made this
worm, he made her like a regular worm wearing a "hat" decorated
with a lot of little tentacles—sorta like strings or
feathers. God didn't give her this "hat" JUST for
decoration though! Her tentacles wave about,
collecting oxygen and food that floats around in the
water current. AND this worm knows how to make a
house by shaping sand into a long tube, half IN the
water, half OUT. Then she crawls into the tube but leaves
her tentacles sticking out (to catch the food and oxygen).
When a bunch of these worms build a bunch of
houses close together, it looks like a whole
neighborhood of feather dusters!

a Feather Duster?

Sometime maybe you will see some of these fancy worms by the seashore, but maybe before then you will see a feather duster. When you do, think about the fancy way God made this little worm—and ALL the fancy kinds of things God made to "decorate" YOUR world. Say a prayer to thank God for letting you live in such a beautiful and fancy-full world!

Color the "feather dusters" pale pink.

Eupolymnia Nebulosa

Don't Bug Out Yet!

Since there are millions or trillions or quintillions of amazing creatures in our buggy world, it would take a VERY long time to learn about ALL of them. You've met a FEW in this book, but there are LOTS more bugs to discover and to learn about. So don't bug out yet!

More Creepy, Crawly, Fuzzy, Funny Facts

- Bugs come in all sizes. Tiny wasps called fairy flies are only one-hundredth of an inch long. Giant stick insects can be 12 inches long.

- Ants always move fast—but they move FASTER when the weather is HOT than they do when it is cool.

- Bees do special dances to tell each other where the best flowers are located.

- The cockroach is one of the oldest types of bugs—it was probably on earth as long as 350 million years ago.

- The bite of a female black widow spider is more deadly than the bite of a rattlesnake!

- Insects are not picky eaters (like SOME kids). They have a VARIED diet. They like to eat some people-food—like fruits and vegetables AND cookies. But they also eat leaves, roots, seeds, bark, dead wood, grain, paper, glue—and other bugs!

- Spiders make webs that are fantastic! They have different patterns and designs, and one web could be made of MILES of silk. This silk is SO strong it may someday be used to cover bulletproof vests!

- The emperor scorpion carries her babies on her back—like people carry babies in backpacks!

- Goliath beetles are truly goliath—they are so big, they weigh as much as hamsters! Although they LOOK scary, they are harmless, and some children in the rain forests of Africa even keep them as pets.

- Bees, wasps, ants, and termites lead a very organized life. Sometimes thousands of them live in one "colony," and each has a special task or job to do—and does it!

In Australia, a family of "processionary" caterpillars will devour all the leaves on an acacia tree and THEN they will all line up, head to tail. Sometimes there will be more than a hundred caterpillars, making a chain 18 feet long! Then off they march, over sand, traveling mostly by night and spinning continuous silk threads to keep the "procession" together. And where are they going? To find another tree to devour!

The Hercules beetle—properly named after the Greek hero, Hercules—has long pointed "horns" that he uses like a forklift to pick up a load of mangoes or bananas. He is seven inches long but can carry a load that weighs as much as five POUNDS. This would be equal to a human who could pick up a fully-loaded dump truck!

The silkworm is a fuzzy white teddy bear of a moth that secretes a fluid which hardens when it touches the air and turns into silk thread. The silkworm then winds the thread into a cocoon. According to history, Lady Hsi-ling-shi, the wife of the Chinese Emperor Huang-ti (who lived more than 2000 years before Christ), was sipping tea in her garden one day when a silkworm's cocoon fell into her cup. When she fished it out, she was shocked to find silky threads. The hot tea had melted the cocoon, and she unrolled a ball of beautiful silk thread. The Chinese began to raise silkworms just to get the cocoons and became the first to make lovely silken clothes out of the silkworm's threads. (It takes 1700 cocoons to make one silk dress!)

Butterflies are sometimes called "flying flowers" because they are so beautiful and come in every color of the rainbow and are decorated with dots, stripes, circles, and many different designs. They might be school-bus-yellow, metallic green, brilliant red, sky blue, purple, orange, or black—BUT they were probably named after the yellow brimstone variety, which are the FIRST to appear in Europe every year and are the exact color of BUTTER!

The most destructive insect in the world is probably the desert locust. It is found in dry areas of Africa, the Middle East, and India. This locust eats its own weight every day. (How much do YOU weigh—60, 70, 100 pounds? Could you eat that much food every day?) A swarm of locusts can destroy a farm, or any place where things are growing, because they can eat 20,000 TONS of vegetation in a day.

Some insects live only a few weeks. Some live only a few hours. But a queen bee might live for seven years, and a queen termite might live even longer.

Some insects are pests, and some are dangerous because they can spread disease. SOME mosquitoes spread malaria. The tsetse fly spreads sleeping sickness. But other insects are very helpful. They eat harmful insects, help maintain an ecological balance in the world, and pollinate plants and flowers.

Earthworms play an important role in recycling and improving soil. As they crawl in and out of the dirt, they "aerate" it and improve the drainage. They continually "mix" the dirt, grinding up leaves and dead plant material and stirring these "nutrients" into the soil. Yards and gardens need these worms so the soil will be rich enough to grow grass, flowers, and vegetables.

People DEPEND on insects to provide us with such things as honey, wax, silk—and chocolate! Bees, butterflies, and other insects fly about taking pollen from one plant to another—and this is the only way plants can produce good things like spices, herbs, fruits, vegetables— and chocolate!

Where Do Bugs Go in the Winter?

Any kind of dead tree stump or old piece of wood makes a good "motel" for bugs to sleep away the winter. You would never know they are there, hiding away. One winter, the folks at a nature museum were making a new display in a glass case and they added an old tree stump. When the heat was turned on in the museum, all sorts of bugs and flying insects woke up, and soon the case was FILLED with swarms of crawling, flying insects. What a surprise! They got a display they had NOT expected. (So don't bring any old wood into YOUR house in the winter or you may be surprised too!)

How Can Bugs Walk on Water?

Some bugs—like the water skaters, springtails, and raft spiders—seem to have magic shoes because they can walk on water! The secret is something called water tension. This is hard to explain, but you can

demonstrate it this way: Take a piece of tissue paper and float it on water. Then place a small needle on the paper. When the paper gets totally water-soaked, the paper will sink—but the needle will still float!

How Can an Insect Be Like a Weatherman?

When you want to know how hot or cold it is outside, do you ever turn on the TV to watch the weatherman or weatherlady tell what the temperature is? Or do you have a thermometer hanging outside so you can check it to find out the temperature? Well, did you know a cricket can also tell you about the temperature? Here's how you can find out: On a summer night when the crickets are chirping, use a stopwatch or the second hand on a watch and COUNT exactly how many times a cricket chirps in one minute. Subtract 40 from that number, divide the answer by 4, and then add 50. For example, if the cricket chirps 60 times in one minute, subtract 40 from 60. This leaves 20. Divide 20 by 4 and you get 5. Add 50—and the temperature should be 55. If the evening is warmer, the cricket will chirp faster and maybe the temperature will be 65 or 75 or 85. Try it and see if it works. (Of course, it is easier to turn on the TV or check the thermometer—but it's not as much fun!)

Some Silly Riddles to "Bug" Your Buddies

What is even more exciting than a talking dog?
A spelling bee!

Why do bees itch?
Because they have hives.

What is the biggest ant?
A gi-ant.

What has eighteen legs and CATCHES flies?
A baseball team.

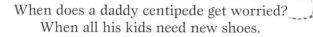

When does a daddy centipede get worried?
When all his kids need new shoes.

What did the mommy lightning bug say to the daddy lightning bug?
Our son sure is bright.

What is a sassy bug?
A cocky roach.

Knock, knock.
Who's there?
Honey bee.
Honey bee who?
Honey, bee nice and get me a cookie.

Knock, knock.
Who's there?
Anna.
Anna who?
Anna long came a spider and sat down beside her.

What is the WORST bug?
A litterbug. (So please don't ever be one!)

What is the BEST worm?
A book worm!

(If YOU are called a book worm because you read so much, it's a compliment!)

Is There Even More to the Life of a Bug?

There are so MANY things to learn about the furry, funny, wiggly, squiggly things God made. After you've read this book, you may want to go to the library and find MORE books about wings, stings, and other things in God's "buggy" world.